FRESH FIRE

90 QUICK READ DEVOTIONALS BOOK ONE

ERIC S. SPEIR

Library of Congress Cataloging-in-Publication data is on file at the Library of Congress, Washington DC.

ISBN: 979-8-9889622-0-5 (paperback)

ISBN: 979-8-9889622-1-2 (ebook)

ALSO BY ERIC S. SPEIR

Grit and Grace: 365 Two-Minute Devotionals

The Struggling Parent: A 30-Day Devotional To Restore Your Hope

Stubborn Faith: 30-Day Devotional For New Growth

To Fellow Disciples
The journey is not easy, but it's worth it!

ACKNOWLEDGMENTS

I have to start by thanking my awesome wife, Roshelle. From her constant encouragement to keep writing when I wanted to give up, she was as important to this book getting done as I was. Thank you so much, dear.

Writing a book is harder than I thought and more rewarding than I could have ever imagined. None of this would have been possible without my editor, Susan Meamber. This is our third book together, and she has once again worked her magic in making me look better than I am.

To my children. I am grateful for each one of you, and I wouldn't want to parent anyone else.

I want to thank God most of all because, without God, I wouldn't be able to do any of this.

INTRODUCTION

What you feed grows, and what you starve dies. If you want to grow your faith, you must feed your faith. Your faith will only be as strong as your devotional life. There's no shortcut to a growing relationship with the Lord. It's built day in and day out by spending time with Him. It's something you must continually tend to and focus on. In the Old Testament, Israel's relationship with the Lord was likened to a fire.

> *The fire on the altar must be kept burning; it must not go out. Every morning the priest is to add firewood and arrange the burnt offering on the fire and burn the fat of the fellowship offerings on it. The fire must be kept burning on the altar continuously; it must not go out.*
> *(Leviticus 6:12-13)*

It's easier to keep a fire going than to start one. To keep a fire going, you must add fresh wood, arrange the wood, tend the wood, and occasionally clean out the ashes. That's a great example of our relationship with the Lord. If we desire to have a fresh encounter with Him, we must add fuel to our fire, and we must be intentional and consistent.

My prayer for you is that, as you read this book, your faith will be ignited and grow. My hope is that you will also be inspired and encouraged along the way. The journey of faith is never easy, but you can rest assured that you are never alone. The Lord is with you, and He wants to speak to you. Come on, get going, and get growing!

1

There's No Line

"Flee the evil desires of youth and pursue righteousness, faith, love and peace, along with those who call on the Lord out of a pure heart." (2 Timothy 2:22)

After working with young adults for so many years, one of the questions they frequently ask is: "Where is the line?" Others have asked, "Is this a sin?" Early on, I would try to define where the line is, but the more I matured, the more I realized it wasn't about being close to a line. It's really about being close to Jesus. When you're close to Jesus, you don't have to worry about where the line is. Instead of asking, "What can I get away with?" start asking, "What can I get away from?"

What temptation or sin do you need to get away from? Ask the Holy Spirit to shine His light on an area of your life where you need to grow or to identify something you need to give up.

2

Don't Settle for Comfort

"One day Terah took his son Abram, his daughter-in-law Sarai (his son Abram's wife), and his grandson Lot (his son Haran's child) and moved away from Ur of the Chaldeans. He was headed for the land of Canaan, but they stopped at Haran and settled there." (Genesis 11:31)

Terah had good intentions of moving his family to the land of Canaan. It was supposed to be a new beginning for them, but along the way, he settled. We don't know why he settled in Haran. It could be that he was grieving the loss of one of his sons. It could have been that he became distracted along the way.

However, we do know that Haran was known as a center of idol worship. Many rabbinical scholars believe that Terah was an idol maker, so it would have been a lucrative opportunity to live and work in a leading capital of idolatry. The struggle might have become too great for him. Either way, Terah settled in his life and quit moving toward his Promised Land.

Your destiny is where you decide to stop. Don't settle for comfort. Keep struggling forward. Where have you settled in your life? Where do you need to pick up and try again?

3

Access Denied

"Guard your heart above all else, for it determines the course of your life"
(Proverbs 4:23).

T he most valuable things in life are guarded. Banks are guarded. Buildings are guarded. If you've ever heard of Fort Knox, you'll instantly be reminded that it's the United States Bullion Depository. It's where all the gold that the federal government owns is stored. It just happens to be next door to the Fort Knox Army base, which is no accident! It's located there because it's being guarded by the most advanced and well-equipped army in the world.

The human heart is more valuable than any amount of gold. It's the workhorse that pumps blood throughout your veins. It's guarded and hidden behind your sternum and rib cage. It's guarded because of its value as the source of life for the body.

The writer of Proverbs understood the value of the heart. He wasn't talking about protecting it physically, but rather spiritually. He was warning us to be careful of who or what we give access to our hearts. Your heart must be guarded from anything that could lead it astray, such as relationships, ideologies, and distractions. Not everything is worth putting your heart into. Be selective and guard your heart, for it determines the course of your life.

4

He's Consistently Consistent

"Jesus Christ is the same yesterday and today and forever." (Hebrews 13:8)

Jesus is consistent and never changes. He doesn't have to change because He's perfect. He's not moody or given to fits of rage or tantrums. He's not up one day and down the next. He's consistently consistent, and because He's consistent, He can be counted on.

Because He is consistent, if He did it once, He can do it again! He still saves. He still heals. He still delivers. He still restores. He still provides. He's still your Lord and King!

I'm not sure what you need today, but He's not running out of miracles. Call out to Him today and allow Him to rescue you and show you how great He is!

Just Keep Quiet

"Fools vent their anger, but the wise quietly hold it back." (Proverbs 29:11)

A person led by their feelings becomes a slave to their circumstances. It's not a sin to be angry. It's a natural response to life and something that God hardwired into every individual. Given the right circumstances, it can be the impetus to make changes or to take a stand. When Jesus walked into the temple and saw how it had been turned into a market, He just didn't pray about it—he flipped tables. That's a great example of righteous anger. (By the way, I'm not giving you permission to go flip tables!)

The key is learning to control your anger. There are times when you need to speak up, and there are times to keep quiet. It's important to know when to keep quiet and when to speak up. Remember, you never have to defend something you don't say. Sometimes it's wise just to keep quiet.

6

Enjoy Every Season

"You set the boundaries of the earth, and you made both summer and winter."
(Psalm 74:17)

E very season of your life is under God's watchful eye. Nothing escapes His attention, and there's nothing that can get past His strong hands. He puts boundaries around your life and protects you. I'm convinced that when we get to heaven, we'll be surprised to discover how much the Lord protected us.

There are good seasons in your life, and there are bad seasons. For the most part, we don't get to decide what season we are in (unless you've made some bad decisions). Even though we can't choose our seasons, we can choose how we go through them. During winter, you often need to put on a coat before you go outside (unless you live in the South, then a Tshirt might just do it!) During a spiritual season of winter, you might have to put on the garment of praise (Isaiah 61:3) and praise your way through the cold season. You can't force a season to change, but you can learn to enjoy the one you're in. Don't let your circumstances dictate your joy, but let your joy guide you through the season you're in.

7

Past Mistakes

"This means that anyone who belongs to Christ has become a new person. The old life is gone; a new life has begun!" (2 Corinthians 5:17)

When you're born again, it's a second chance at life. It's a chance to start fresh and get a do-over. You can't change your past, but you can change your future. Your past is in the past, so don't let it determine your future. You need to forgive yourself and then move on. Your past gets a voice, not a vote. Learn from your past, but don't plan your future around it.

Where do you need to forgive yourself or let something go? What's keeping you from becoming a new person in Christ?

8

You're Not The Only One

"Stand firm against him, and be strong in your faith. Remember that your family of believers all over the world is going through the same kind of suffering you are." (1 Peter 5:9)

It's easy to get stuck in our struggles and think we are the only ones going through pain and difficulty. The enemy wants to single you out and isolate you. If he can get you to think that you're the only one facing painful challenges, then he can get you to give up. In reality, you're not the only one facing suffering.

Jesus was no stranger to suffering (Isaiah 53:3). Likewise, the Christian life is a life of suffering. If Jesus suffered, then we should expect no less. The good news is that we can have confidence that Jesus not only sees but also understands us. If you're suffering today, I want to remind you that you're not the only one; Jesus has been there. You can have confidence that He will comfort you and give you peace amid your pain. You can also rest in knowing God can turn any situation around. He did it in three days for Jesus, and He can do the same for you!

9

Preparation and Opportunity

"Take a lesson from the ants, you lazybones. Learn from their ways and become wise! Though they have no prince or governor or ruler to make them work, they labor hard all summer, gathering food for the winter." (Proverbs 6:6- 8)

Ants understand the seasons of life. They understand that the best time to prepare for winter is in the summer. If you wait until winter to prepare for the cold, it's too late. They use the good seasons to prepare for the difficult ones.

I would also add that it's easier to stay prepared than it is to get ready. Many people miss opportunities because they wait to prepare until they have an opportunity. Opportunities usually come to the prepared! It takes faith to prepare for an opportunity. What opportunity should you be preparing for?

Possible Impossibilities

"He replied, 'What is impossible for people is possible for God.'" (Luke 18:27)

F aith is not an "easy button" in life. It's the difference maker between the natural and the supernatural. When you have faith, you're inviting the presence of Jesus into your life and circumstances. If you've read the Gospels, you'll realize that anything becomes possible when Jesus steps into the situation. For instance, Jesus wrecked every funeral He attended by raising the dead—because He is the resurrection and the life. Dead things can't stay down when He's around! Faith doesn't make things easy; it makes things possible.

Where in your life do you need Jesus to make something possible? Take a moment and pray to Him and ask for a miracle.

11

Power Needs Character

"You intended to harm me, but God intended it all for good. He brought me to this position so I could save the lives of many people." (Genesis 50:20)

I magine being sold into slavery by your brothers, then being falsely accused and thrown into prison. This is what happened to Joseph, and he ended up as a slave for Potiphar. A few years later, he would be exonerated and promoted to the second highest position in Egypt. He would also face his brothers who instigated all the pain in his life. I'm sure it took a lot of time in prayer to overcome the pain people inflicted on his life and to forgive all the people who hurt him.

Joseph passed the greatest test of character when he chose not to use his position to get even with those who had unjustifiably injured him. He could have taken vengeance on Potiphar, but he didn't. He could have thrown his brothers into prison, but he didn't. Instead, he used his power to save others. Few people can handle this much power!

12

The Fire that Brings Promotion

"Then the king promoted Shadrach, Meshach, and Abednego to even higher positions in the province of Babylon." (Daniel 3:30)

E veryone wants a promotion, but few people want to go through the fire to get them. The three Hebrew children were thrown into the fire for their faith. They defied the king's orders to bow down and worship the idol, resulting in them being thrown into the fire.

Maybe you're in the fire today for trying to do the right thing. Your fire might be a messy divorce or a challenging job situation. You might be in the fire today, but you're not alone. There is a fourth man, and He's with you. Testing precedes promotion. What the enemy meant to destroy you, God will use to elevate you.

13

You Can't Take it with You

"Do not store up for yourselves treasures on earth, where moths and vermin destroy, and where thieves break in and steal. But store up for yourselves treasures in heaven, where moths and vermin do not destroy, and where thieves do not break in and steal. For where your treasure is, there your heart will be also." (Matthew 6:19-21)

This verse is not talking about not having savings or investing money for retirement. It's talking about the accumulation of stuff. As Americans, we like our stuff. Look at most people's garages. Our garages are so full that we can't park our cars in them. Some people have so much that they rent space to store their stuff. In America, the storage business is a billion-dollar industry.

God doesn't mind if you have stuff as long as stuff doesn't have you.

We need to find the balance between having stuff we don't need and having enough.

I've done several funerals over the years, and I've never seen a U-Haul attached to a hearse. You can't take your treasure with you, but you can send it ahead of you. When you're generous and give to the Lord, you're storing up treasures in heaven.

14

Plant a Bigger Garden

"Remember this—a farmer who plants only a few seeds will get a small crop. But the one who plants generously will get a generous crop. You must decide in your heart how much to give. And don't give reluctantly or in response to pressure. 'For God loves a person who gives cheerfully.'" (*2 Corinthians 9:6-7*)

Several years ago, my wife and I planted a garden. Truthfully, I wanted a garden, but she did not. She understood the work it would take to keep it up. I underestimated this process and went a little heavy on the seed. Our idea of a small garden turned into a big harvest.

I learned a few lessons from this experience. First, you get to decide the size of your crop. If you want a larger harvest, plant more seeds. Second, you get to choose your seed. Finally, you'll only get a harvest after the seeds are sown.

If you have a need today, plant some seeds in fertile ground.

15

The Seeds of Life

"Those who live only to satisfy their own sinful nature will harvest decay and death from that sinful nature. But those who live to please the Spirit will harvest everlasting life from the Spirit." (Galatians 6:8)

Your life harvest is determined by the seeds you sow. When you live to please the Spirit, you'll reap a harvest of righteousness and blessing. Over the years, I've been constantly shocked at the number of people who have been angry at God for the choices they've made. You are free to choose, but you are not free from the consequences of your choices. Your life is perfectly designed for the results you are getting. If you don't like your results, change your life.

16

Disciple Your Children

"And you must commit yourselves wholeheartedly to these commands that I am giving you today. Repeat them again and again to your children. Talk about them when you are at home and when you are on the road, when you are going to bed and when you are getting up." (Deuteronomy 6:6-7)

There's never been a more challenging time to raise children. The world is not getting any easier; it seems to be viler by the day. Now more than ever, parents need to be intentional about discipling their children. It doesn't have to be complicated. You don't have to sit around and have an hour-long Bible study together every night. It could be as short and simple as taking a walk together or tucking them in at night. Also, prayers don't have to be long to be effective. They just need to be spoken. So often, more is caught than taught. Don't be afraid to model the behavior that you expect out of your children.

If you don't disciple your children, someone else will. Be careful what you let them be exposed to. Don't believe the enemy's lie that your children are not listening to you. You are the most important and influential person in their life. Don't leave their eternity to chance.

17

May Hope Arise

"Now all glory to God, who is able, through his mighty power at work within us, to accomplish infinitely more than we might ask or think." (Ephesians 3:20)

There's an old boxing adage that says, "It's the punch that you don't see coming that knocks you out." Life has a way of knocking the wind out of us. Life is full of disappointments. We live in a fallen world with fallen people. At some point in time, we are going to face disappointments.

If we aren't careful, we will allow the disappointments in life to determine our faith and expectations. The good news is that when you're a born-again believer, you have a power within you that is working on your behalf. The Holy Spirit resides in your life, and when He's within you, anything becomes possible. Don't lower your expectations; raise your hopes!

18

Your Thoughts Matter

"But that isn't what you learned about Christ. Since you have heard about Jesus and have learned the truth that comes from him, throw off your old sinful nature and your former way of life, which is corrupted by lust and deception. Instead, let the Spirit renew your thoughts and attitudes. Put on your new nature, created to be like God—truly righteous and holy." (Ephesians 4:20-24)

In these verses, the Apostle Paul encouraged the Ephesian believers to allow the Holy Spirit to transform and renew their minds. Many of these Ephesian believers had grown up in and around idolatry. Before coming to Christ, they had believed lies and had carnal thinking. They lived sinful lives because of their sinful thoughts.

Paul also wrote, "And now, dear brothers and sisters, one final thing. Fix your thoughts on what is true, and honorable, and right, and pure, and lovely, and admirable. Think about things that are excellent and worthy of praise" (Philippians 4:8).

Paul understood that the only way to change your life is to change your thoughts. Your thoughts become renewed the more time you spend in the Word and the more time you spend in the presence of the Lord. Remember, change your thoughts; change your life.

19

Don't Lose Your Way

"But when Rehoboam was firmly established and strong, he abandoned the Law of the Lord, and all Israel followed him in this sin." (2 Chronicles 12:1)

The most dangerous time in a person's life is when things are too comfortable. A life without resistance is a life without the need for God. King Rehoboam learned this lesson the hard way. When Rehoboam first became king, he was desperate for God's help. He knew he couldn't do it by himself, but the more God blessed him, the easier things became, and the more he relied on his own abilities.

If we are not careful, the blessings of God can complicate our lives. That's why staying humble and hungry for the Lord is essential.

20

Faith and Work

"Just as the body is dead without breath, so also faith is dead without good works."
(James 2:26)

It's important to have faith. The supernatural can happen when faith and work team up together. Faith is the "super," and work is the "natural." When you do the natural, then God will do the super. The key is for you to work, so God has something with which to work. He cannot bless what you're not doing!

Too many times, I've prayed and asked the Lord to bless something in my life, and He has often reminded me that I must do my part first. Almost anything we do for the Lord is going to require some risk and faith on our part. This is usually expressed through work. When we work, then God works.

Where have you been afraid to take a step of faith in your life? God never asked you to take a leap of faith; He's only asked you to take a step of faith. What's one step you could take toward Him today?

21

Past Mistakes

"No, dear brothers and sisters, I have not achieved it, but I focus on this one thing: Forgetting the past and looking forward to what lies ahead, I press on to reach the end of the race and receive the heavenly prize for which God, through Christ Jesus, is calling us." (Philippians 3:13-14)

The Apostle Paul's story did not start off well. He started off as a religious zealot who thought he was doing God a favor by having Christians killed and imprisoned. He was there when the crowd stoned Stephen. In fact, he was the one holding their jackets and encouraging them to cast the stones. He saw others beaten and imprisoned. It's hard to imagine how these thoughts would try to come back later and haunt his memories. If Paul understood anything, it was the grace and forgiveness of God. That's what makes these verses so powerful. Paul learned to forgive himself, forget the past, and look forward to what lay ahead.

Your past is just a story. It doesn't have to be the narrator of your future. Where do you need to forgive yourself?

22

Ordinary Miracles

"So Naaman went down to the Jordan River and dipped himself seven times, as the man of God had instructed him. And his skin became as healthy as the skin of a young child, and he was healed!" (2 Kings 5:14)

E lisha, the prophet, commanded Naaman to go down to the Jordan River and dip himself seven times so that he would be healed. There wasn't anything special about the Jordan River. By outward appearances, it was shallow and dirty. The miracle was in the obedience, not the river. It takes perseverance to keep doing something even when you do not see immediate results. Naaman had to dip himself seven times before he saw his miracle.

What would have happened if he had stopped at the sixth time and given up? This is a great reminder to keep pushing through until you see the breakthrough. Keep showing up. Keep praying. Keep giving. Keep speaking faith. Keep on keeping on. There's a miracle on the seventh time around!

23

Hold it Back

"Fools vent their anger, but the wise quietly hold it back." (Proverbs 29:11)

You'll never have to apologize for something you don't say. It's best to keep quiet until you're able to have a civil conversation than to speak from your pain. I've often spoken out of anger and, in the process, done damage to my loved ones and to my relationships.

This verse also reminds you that you shouldn't vent your life to everyone around you. Some people in your life can't handle your pain. For example, if you're married, you should vent to your spouse, not dump your feelings on your children. Children don't have the emotional capacity and maturity to carry the weight of your pain. Let's leave that to your spouse or to a trusted friend or mentor.

24

It's an Inside Job

"But the Holy Spirit produces this kind of fruit in our lives: love, joy, peace, patience, kindness, goodness, faithfulness, gentleness, and self-control. There is no law against these things!" (Galatians 5:22-23)

People often confuse the fruit of the Spirit with a feeling. Joy is a spiritual fruit, not a feeling. Don't wait for your feelings to catch up with your spirit. Joy is an inside job. It's not dependent upon your circumstances or on those around you. It's a daily choice to live in gratitude and thankfulness for what God has done and is doing in your life. You can practice joy today by taking a few minutes to thank God for His goodness in your life. Go ahead and try it! Invite the Holy Spirit right where you are to come and fill you with joy.

25

Emmanuel

"Look! The virgin will conceive a child! She will give birth to a son, and they will call him Immanuel, which means 'God is with us.'" (Matthew 1:23)

When Joseph received this promise in a dream, it was a new revelation for him. The Israelites had endured the last 400 years in silence from the Lord, but He was about to do something new. No longer would Israel try to find a way to Him, He was going to make a way to them.

When you're walking through hardship or difficulty, it's too easy to buy the lie that God has left you or abandoned you. The Bible never promises us exemption from problems, but it does promise us One who walks with us through them. Emmanuel is God with us. He's with you today. Don't be afraid to call out to Him and invite Him into your situation. He's the God of miracles, and there's nothing He cannot do!

26

Monuments or Footprints

"Early the next morning Samuel went to find Saul. Someone told him, 'Saul went to the town of Carmel to set up a monument to himself; then he went on to Gilgal.'" (1 Samuel 15:12)

In life, you can either leave monuments or footprints. Monuments show what you've done. Footprints show how far you've come. Monuments are about making a name for yourself. Footprints are about leaving a path for others to follow. Footprints are about leaving a legacy of faith for others to follow. Your footprints might just be the courage others need to see. Someone behind you just needs to see that it can be done. If God can do it for you, He can do it for them! Choose to keep moving because someone needs to see your courage.

27

Be a Dreamer

"His brothers responded, 'So you think you will be our king, do you? Do you actually think you will reign over us?' And they hated him all the more because of his dreams and the way he talked about them." (Genesis 37:8)

Not everyone wants to hear your dreams. Unfortunately, there are too many people in our lives who don't understand our calling or who don't believe in us. Even worse, it's usually those closest to us that believe in us the least. Even Jesus was despised in his own hometown, and He couldn't do many miracles because of their unbelief (Mark 6:4-6). If people didn't believe in Jesus, then you're in good company.

It's also important to show wisdom and not share your dreams with everyone. Truthfully, not everyone has the faith you do, and they can't handle people like you. People who don't dream despise those who do.

Don't share your dreams with just anyone. Make sure the person is qualified to hear your dreams!

Don't Fool Yourself

"Don't be fooled by those who say such things, for 'bad company corrupts good character.'" (1 Corinthians 15:33)

Don't fool yourself. You're probably not as strong as you think. Your relationships matter. Association brings assimilation. Who you follow will determine who you become.

You can associate with others, but you don't have to assimilate with them. When you assimilate with others, you conform to their ideas and values. You become like the people with whom you hang out. Don't allow some of the people around you to change who you are.

If you want to grow stronger in your faith, hang out with or listen to people who are stronger in the faith than you. I've gotten stronger as I've spent time with people who are stronger than me. They have pushed me to grow stronger and to keep pursuing progress. I am not where I was, but I am not who I used to be.

29

There are No Shortcuts

"Lazy people want much but get little, but those who work hard will prosper."
(Proverbs 13:4)

Don't believe every post on social media. The clearest path to prosperity is through hard work. There are no shortcuts to prosperity. You can have talent, but without the accompanying work ethic, you're doomed to be average.

In the famous race between the tortoise and the hare, the tortoise always beats the hare because a consistent person will eventually surpass a lazy but talented person. The consistent person has learned to keep showing up when others quit. If you keep showing up, you'll be the only person left standing. That's how you pass your competition.

30

The Roots Precede the Fruit

"I am the vine; you are the branches. If you remain in me and I in you, you will bear much fruit; apart from me you can do nothing." (John 15:5)

We live in a society that is afraid of commitment. Many young people are choosing to get married later in life because they've experienced the pain of broken promises, broken marriages, and broken homes. It's no wonder people are afraid to commit to long-term plans.

As hard as it is to commit to things in life, it's important to do it anyway. Every committed believer wants to bear fruit, but few want to put down roots. You'll never see fruit if you don't put down roots. The only way to bear fruit in your life is to stay connected to the vine. It requires a commitment of faith and staying in one place long enough to see transformation in your life. That's why it's important to be tied to and committed to a local church. When you connect to like-minded believers, you will grow in discipleship and maturity. The key is putting down roots in your life. The only way to put down roots is to plant yourself some-where and become unmovable by your circumstances and feelings.

31

Believing in Miracles

"I ask you again, does God give you the Holy Spirit and work miracles among you because you obey the law? Of course not! It is because you believe the message you heard about Christ." (Galatians 3:5)

You can't earn a miracle. There's no amount of keeping the law of the Lord that can earn you anything. The way to a miracle is through believing. It's that simple!

The world teaches that seeing is believing, but in God's Kingdom, we understand that believing is seeing. Paul encourages the Galatians by helping them understand that seeing a miracle starts with believing it is possible through faith in Jesus Christ. If you need a miracle today, call out to Jesus and see what He will do! Go ahead; He's waiting to hear from you!

32

Turning Points

"And we know that in all things God works for the good of those who love him, who have been called according to his purpose." (Romans 8:28)

G od can turn your disappointments into turning points when you trust Him. At some point in life, everyone is going to face a crushing disappointment. It might be the loss of a job, or maybe your child wanders from the faith or makes a poor decision. It could be a financial crisis. No one is immune to disappointments, but for the believer, that does not mark the end of the story. When we love Him and are called according to His purposes, not our own, we can believe in a turning point in every situation we face in life.

The promise we have is that He can work for good in all things in our lives. The Scripture doesn't say some things. It says ALL things!

33

Don't Belittle People

"It is a sin to belittle one's neighbor; blessed are those who help the poor."
(Proverbs 14:21)

To belittle someone means to make someone feel unimportant. An easier way to say this is to make someone be or feel little. If you have to make yourself bigger by making someone feel little, then you're doing it wrong.

Every day, we have an opportunity to change someone's life with our words. All it takes to change the trajectory of someone's day is to speak a kind or encouraging word to them. It's important that we speak up to people, not down to them. Don't expect people to live up to their potential if you talk down to them.

34

Be Steadfast

"Therefore, my beloved brothers, be steadfast, immovable, always abounding in the work of the Lord, knowing that in the Lord your labor is not in vain."
(*1 Corinthians 15:58*)

A few years ago, while I was working on my doctorate, one of my mentors shared something that I have never forgotten. It came at just the right time because I'm a recovering perfectionist. Maybe you are too. I was struggling to write my dissertation, and he said to me, "It doesn't have to be perfect; it just has to be done." These words became my mantra for the next year and a half. I repeated them over and over to myself, and I learned that it's more important to be focused on progress, not perfection.

I learned that consistency beats intensity. As long as you keep showing up, then you can accomplish just about anything. As long as you're steadfast and immovable in your pursuits, then you'll be unstoppable!

Lonely Places

"But Jesus often withdrew to lonely places and prayed." (Luke 5:16)

You're only as strong as your prayer life. Praying can sometimes be lonely work. The church prayer meeting is arguably one of the most important meetings of the week but the least attended. The prayer closet can be lonely, but it's the place where things get done.

If Jesus had to withdraw to pray and seek His Father, then there's a good chance we need to do it as well. If the Son of God doesn't get a free pass from prayer, then we need to follow in His footsteps. It's not that we have to, it's that we need to. I would venture to say that the prayer closet was Jesus' secret sauce to a life of miracles and breakthroughs. You're one prayer away from a different life!

Walk Through Walls

"... and the Israelites went through the sea on dry ground, with a wall of water on their right and on their left." (Exodus 14:22)

The Israelites found themselves between a rock and a hard place. They were facing a wall of water on one side and the Egyptian army closing in on the other side. In their panic, they cried out to the Lord because it looked like He brought them to a dead end, but a dead end is only the end when you stop moving. When God is guiding your life, there are no dead ends. Any step He leads you to can be a new beginning. Finally, if God can bring you to it, He can bring you through it.

You might be facing a wall in your life, but don't panic. If God brought you there, He can take you to the next place. If God has to, He can make you walk through walls.

Double Portions

"When they came to the other side, Elijah said to Elisha, 'Tell me what I can do for you before I am taken away.' And Elisha replied, 'Please let me inherit a double share of your spirit and become your successor.'" (2 Kings 2:9)

Up until this point in the story, Elisha had not done one single miracle. He was known as the "one who poured water on the hands of Elijah" (2 Kings 3:11). In other words, he was the dishwasher! He had spent years with Elijah watching him perform miracle after miracle, but he had not done one himself. Truthfully, he was serving, studying, and giving. By outward appearances, it probably looked like a wasted season in his life. However, it wasn't a wasted season; it was a season of preparation. He knew eventually that if he kept serving, he would have his day, and he would be ready when the day came.

When the day came, the only thing Elisha wanted was a double portion of Elijah's spirit. He simply wanted Elijah's mantle of anointing. Elisha knew that if he was going to do something he'd never done before, he would need something he had never had before. (Read that last statement again!) You can't keep doing what you've always done and expect new results.

Finally, new seasons require new anointing. What worked in the last season won't be enough for the new season God is taking you into. It's going to require more of you!

38

The Extravagance of God

"He also made seven lamps for the lampstand, lamp snuffers, and trays, all of pure gold. The entire lampstand, along with its accessories, was made from 75 pounds of pure gold." (Exodus 37:23-24).

Today gold is worth $1,806 an ounce. With just a little bit of math, we realize the lampstand would cost $2,167,200 to make today. I don't know about you, but that's a lot of cabbage to make a lampstand!

Back then, gold was also the most highly valued commodity. It seems God was a bit extravagant here, but it's only extravagant if you're limited in resources. If God can do this, then there's no limit to what He can do in your life!

Identity Matters

"Jesus knew that the Father had given him authority over everything and that he had come from God and would return to God. So he got up from the table, took off his robe, wrapped a towel around his waist, and poured water into a basin. Then he began to wash the disciples' feet, drying them with the towel he had around him." (John 13:3-5)

Jesus never forgot where He came from. He knew He was royalty. Regardless of where he found himself, Jesus would not change who He was. He exchanged his royal robes of heaven for the towel as an example for us to follow. Nothing was beneath Jesus because He was confident in His identity.

Your identity is based on what God says about you, not on positions or other people's opinions. When you know who called you and where you came from, then serving is not beneath you. Your position does not determine or diminish your identity.

40

Ask for Another Gift

"She said, 'Let me have another gift. You have already given me land in the Negev; now please give me springs of water, too.' So Caleb gave her the upper and lower springs." (Judges 1:15)

I have always struggled with this verse. Truthfully, I never fully understood it. Caleb's daughter received land as an inheritance. As a female, living in a patriarchal society, this was unusual. Women typically did not receive land as an inheritance, but this situation was different. Not only was she given land, but she was also bold enough to ask for another gift. She wanted springs of living water to go with it. She wasn't satisfied with a piece of land. She wanted all that her father was willing to give her. All she had to do was be bold enough to ask.

In the New Testament, Jesus promised the disciples a gift by His father. In Acts 1:4, Jesus told his disciples "to wait for the gift" that the Father had promised. In Joel 2, the gift was promised to men, women, children, and anyone who would ask for it.

All these verses refer to the Holy Spirit. The Father is willing to give you another gift today; all you have to do is ask for it. I would encourage you to take a few minutes and ask the Father for the gift of His Holy Spirit. He will change your life.

Keep Knocking

"Next Paul and Silas traveled through the area of Phrygia and Galatia, because the Holy Spirit had prevented them from preaching the word in the province of Asia at that time. Then coming to the borders of Mysia, they headed north for the province of Bithynia, but again the Spirit of Jesus did not allow them to go there. So instead, they went on through Mysia to the seaport of Troas. That night Paul had a vision: A man from Macedonia in northern Greece was standing there, pleading with him. 'Come over to Macedonia and help us!' So we decided to leave for Macedonia at once, having concluded that God was calling us to preach the Good News there." (Acts 16:6-10)

P aul and Silas traveled through Phrygia and Galatia because the Holy Spirit prevented them from preaching the word in Asia. They tried to go through Bithynia, but again the Spirit of Jesus did not allow them to go there. I suspect Paul experienced frustration because he was trying to do the will of God, but at every turn, he faced obstacles. The problem was that the obstacles were from Jesus! Later, Paul had a vision and received a call from the man of Macedonia in northern Greece, and concluded that God was calling them to preach the Good News there.

Paul was obviously disappointed that the Lord would not allow him to enter Asia. Two times he tried a door, and two times the Spirit of Jesus would not allow him. Sometimes you're trying to do the right thing, but things don't work out. Occasionally something fails, and you do not have a good reason for it. When these moments happen, we have to trust that Jesus has other plans for us. It will require us to get back up and knock on doors. If we let Him, God can turn our disappointments into new appointments

42

You Need To Fess Up

"Samson said, 'This time I cannot be blamed for everything I am going to do to you Philistines.'" (Judges 15:3)

S amson was his own worst enemy. Time and time again, he refused to take responsibility for his actions. Because of Samson's lack of self-control and reluctance to take responsibility, he started a tit-for-tat war with the Philistines. It grew progressively worse until the Philistines came and settled in Lehi to capture Samson. The saddest part of this story is that it resulted in Samson losing his vision and, eventually, his life.

If you don't learn to take responsibility for your life, you'll never become the person God wants you to be. We can't control what others do to us, but we can control our response. That's the only thing we can control. The best way to start taking responsibility for your life is by admitting when you're wrong or when you've made a mistake. You grow up when you start to fess up!

43

Lulled To Sleep

"Delilah lulled Samson to sleep with his head in her lap, and then she called in a man to shave off the seven locks of his hair. In this way she began to bring him down, and his strength left him." (Judges 16:19)

Samson's downfall didn't happen overnight. It happened little by little until his mistress had lulled him to sleep. Samson was oblivious to this tactic. If it had required a fight, Samson would have indeed won, but this fight was more subtle. Samson's downfall started with being in a relationship he should not have been in. In his arrogance, he thought he could handle it and that the rules did not apply to him. He laid his head in the enemy's lap, and it ended up costing him his life and calling.

The enemy still operates this way today. He does not come at us head on. He often gets us to compromise in a small area of our life. Once we compromise in one area, it leads us to another area and then another.

Before you know it, you have been lulled to sleep, and you find yourself in a position you never imagined.

Be careful because association brings assimilation. Guard your mind and thoughts. If you are stuck today, I encourage you to cry out to the Holy Spirit to set you free. God's grace is here for those who cry out to Him.

44

Vision Loss

"Then Delilah said, 'You've been making fun of me and telling me lies! Now tell me how you can be tied up securely.'" (Judges 16:13)

Samson started in a place and in a relationship in which he should not have engaged. The relationship started with a few small lies. Truth be told, Samson thought it was a joke and laughed it off. He kept mocking and flirting with the truth. Samson started by telling one lie, but then he had to keep lying. He kept going until he found himself bound by the enemy, who poked out his eyes. In the end, he lost his vision because he kept telling lies.

Satan does the same in our lives. He gets us to tell one lie, then another, and then another. Before we know it, we've embraced the lies, and it ends up costing us our vision. When we lose our vision, we lose our way.

45

Never Underestimate Obedience

"Because one person disobeyed God, many became sinners. But because one other person obeyed God, many will be made righteous." (Romans 5:19)

My wife's entire family serves the Lord because one man responded to the Lord for salvation. My wife's grandfather was a teenager when an evangelist came to town and set up a tent for revival services. Out of curiosity, he went to see what the men were doing. They witnessed to him, and he gave his heart to the Lord. He was the first new convert in a fledgling church. Years later, he became a pastor. His granddaughter, who is my wife, would be saved, and eventually, we would serve on staff at the church where her grandfather got saved! Years later, I would spend most of my ministry training young men and women for full-time ministry. The actions of one man changed his destiny and his family tree. God can do the same for you. All you have to do is decide to surrender to Him today.

Never underestimate one act of disobedience in your life. It could influence more than just you. Likewise, never underestimate one act of obedience. It might just change the world. If not, it could just change your world.

46

Servant Leadership

"Then Elkanah returned home to Ramah without Samuel. And the boy served the Lord by assisting Eli the priest." (1 Samuel 2:11)

Samuel's job was to assist Eli, the priest. Eli was old, overweight, and had just about lost his vision. Quite possibly, Eli could not do things easily, so Samuel did all the grunt work and the menial tasks at the Tabernacle. Truthfully, Eli had all but disqualified himself from leadership because he failed to confront the sin of his sons, who were priests. Hophni and Phineas stole the best offerings and had sex with women as they came to make sacrifices. They did not exemplify godly spiritual leadership. Despite his environment, Samuel served well.

Although Eli almost disqualified himself from the priesthood, Samuel still chose to honor and serve him without becoming proud because of his position or allowing it to go to his head or heart. He learned to serve through leadership, not around it. If you find yourself waiting for your turn, it's important to remember that you serve through leadership, not around it.

47

Be the Doorkeeper

"Samuel stayed in bed until morning, then got up and opened the doors of the Tabernacle as usual. He was afraid to tell Eli what the Lord had said to him."
(*1 Samuel 3:15*)

S amuel was a remarkable young man. The morning after the Lord spoke to him prophetically, Samuel got up and went to work as usual. He was hesitant to tell Eli what the Lord had said to him. He could have arrogantly blurted out what the Lord had told him, were it not for his servant heart. He could have assumed that he was a rising star who needed a big platform from which to speak. Instead, he went to work as usual as the doorkeeper. Samuel kept serving and doing what the Lord had called him to do. How's that for a servant's heart?

Samuel kept being the doorkeeper until the Lord opened a door for him. The best way to avoid knocking on the wrong door is to let the Lord open it for you. You'll never have to knock on an open door.

48

Temporary Seasons

"Nevertheless, that time of darkness and despair will not go on forever. The land of Zebulun and Naphtali will be humbled, but there will be a time in the future when Galilee of the Gentiles, which lies along the road that runs between the Jordan and the sea, will be filled with glory." (Isaiah 9:1)

God established seasons at creation, and every season has its purpose. Every season has a scheduled end. You might be going through a time of darkness and despair, but the Lord's promise to you is that it will not go on forever.

You might be living in between seasons but know it's only temporary. Eventually, the storms will break, and the dawn will come with the rising of the sun. Your season of difficulty has an expiration date. In the meantime, keep on keeping on!

49

God's Purposes Prevail

"After the Lord has used the king of Assyria to accomplish his purposes on Mount Zion and in Jerusalem, he will turn against the king of Assyria and punish him— for he is proud and arrogant." (Isaiah 10:12)

The Lord used the king of Assyria to accomplish His plans for the life of Israel. This thought might bother you, but the Lord is sovereign and is in control. He can use anyone, including your enemies, to accomplish His purposes for your life.

I once worked for a manager who was not a believer and was not known as a generous person. I had been at the job for a while and had earned a raise, but the manager would not give me the raise, so I kept praying about it. Eventually, he gave me a raise and a company gas card to help with travel expenses. As he gave it to me, he said, "I am not even sure why I'm doing this! I feel like I'm just supposed to do it." In the end, I know it's because I prayed, and the Holy Spirit moved on his heart to bless my life.

God can do the same for you! He can use people in unusual ways to bless your life. It can come from unexpected places and in unexpected ways.

50

When All Else Fails

"But while knowledge makes us feel important, it is love that strengthens the church. Anyone who claims to know all the answers doesn't really know very much. But the person who loves God is the one whom God recognizes."
(1 Corinthians 8:1-3)

These verses are pretty straightforward. Knowledge makes us feel important and powerful. While knowledge is important, it is useless unless it is grounded in love. God is not impressed with our knowledge. Knowledge doesn't get His attention, but love does. Loving others will get the attention of heaven on your life, and when the attention of heaven is on your life, anything is possible. When all else fails, try love!

51

Stay Planted

"Wise old craftsmen from Gebal did the caulking. Ships from every land came with goods to barter for your trade." (Ezekiel 27:9)

I n this chapter, the prophet Ezekiel describes the city of Tyre. It was a beautiful and prosperous city. At one time, it was the trading center of the world. It was a city known not only for its trade, but also for its shipbuilding. The seaside location provided a natural location for the shipping industry to thrive and prosper.

In this verse, the Lord talks about Tyre's famous reputation for shipbuilding. This lucrative business required skilled labor. Caulking, the most important task of the shipbuilders, was critical because, if not done correctly, the ship would sink, and all the men and cargo would be lost. Such an important task could not be placed in the hands of a novice, but rather delegated to the most trusted and experienced craftsman.

Our culture celebrates youth. Conversely, our cultural tends to shun the older generation for being out of touch. In reality, the world needs their experience. One's physical strength and beauty might wane with age, but the experience of the older generation is invaluable.

Even the business world recognizes the need for wisdom and experience. Since 2000, over 58% of S&P 500 CEOs have been between the ages of 50-59. In fact, across all industries, the average age of a CEO is 59 years of age.

As believers, we can live with the promise that our age does not limit us. Psalm 92:14 says, "Even in old age they will still produce fruit; they will remain vital and green." God's desire is for you to keep producing fruit with your life. As long as you stay planted, you will always stay vital and green to those around you.

52

Go the Extra Mile

"If a soldier demands that you carry his gear for a mile, carry it two miles."
(Matthew 5:41)

It doesn't take make much to stand out from the crowd right now. All you have to do to stand out is be willing to do a little more than the person beside you. Average people go one mile, while champions go two miles. Choose the extra mile. There's no competition on the extra mile.

53

Work at It

"Work at living in peace with everyone, and work at living a holy life, for those who are not holy will not see the Lord." (Hebrews 12:14)

There will be times in your life when you will not get along with everyone. Some people will not like you simply because you have the Holy Spirit living in your life. When that happens, do your best to live in peace with them. You can't control how they treat you, but you can control your response. When this happens, you must discipline yourself and deny your flesh. It might mean choosing not to respond in anger when this person crosses or mistreats you. It takes work to get along with people you don't like.

54

Know Your Why

"For the joy set before him he endured the cross, scorning its shame, and sat down at the right hand of the throne of God." (Hebrews 12:2)

When you know your why, you won't lose your way. Life is hard, and you will face times when you want to quit! In those moments, circle back to your calling, but this requires that you know why you do what you do.

Jesus' why kept Him on the cross. He kept looking forward to a future time of joy. He understood that the pain was temporary. Jesus could endure the cross because He could see past His temporary pain. He knew a throne was just on the other side of the cross. He looked forward to the Marriage Supper of the Lamb when all believers would gather around His table to celebrate the consummation of the Kingdom.

When you have a strong why, you can endure just about anything. What is your why? What compels you to keep going when you feel like giving up?

55

When You're Stuck

"While Jeremiah was still confined in the courtyard of the guard, the Lord gave him this second message: 'This is what the Lord says—the Lord who made the earth, who formed and established it, whose name is the Lord: Ask me and I will tell you remarkable secrets you do not know about things to come.'"
(Jeremiah 33:1-3).

Jeremiah was stuck. He was in a place that he did not want to be in. He didn't sign up for what he was going through. He never asked for trouble, but trouble found him. For whatever reason, the Lord placed him there for a season. Jeremiah did nothing to deserve being imprisoned by the king. He wasn't living an openly sinful life, and neither was God judging him for his sins. Even though he was imprisoned in a place where he didn't want to be, God still spoke to him and gave him a message.

In the midst of seclusion and confinement in a difficult place, the Lord spoke to Jeremiah and told him to ask Him about secret things to come. Seclusion is God's invitation for intimacy. If you're feeling secluded today, don't waste it. Invite God into your mess, and He can make a miracle out of it!

56

Just Believe

"Then Jesus said, 'Did I not tell you that if you believe, you will see the glory of God?'" (John 11:40)

F aith does not deny your reality; it helps you to get through it. There will be moments when God delivers you from a storm, and there will be times when He delivers you through it. During these times, it's going to require you to muster your faith and believe God for the outcome.

If you do the natural, God will do the supernatural. Your response to a crisis is to have faith in God. When you believe in Him, you can rest assured that you will see the glory of God in your life. He can move any mountain before you. If He doesn't take you over it, then He can take you through it. Your job is to "faith it" until you make it.

No Dead Ends

"Now I am deeply discouraged, but I will remember you—even from distant Mount Hermon, the source of the Jordan, from the land of Mount Mizar. I hear the tumult of the raging seas as your waves and surging tides sweep over me. But each day the Lord pours his unfailing love upon me, and through each night I sing his songs, praying to God who gives me life." (Psalm 42:6-8)

Apparently, the psalmist was deeply discouraged. He fought discouragement in the present by remembering what God had done in his past. The greatest predictor of future behavior is past behavior. If God has been good to you once, then He will be good to you again.

If you're discouraged today, you need to pull out your journal or a sheet of prayer and write down the moments when God has come through for you. When has He provided for you in the past? When has He healed you? When has He delivered or protected you? If He did it once, He can do it again.

58

Wait for It

"'No!' David said. 'Don't kill him. For who can remain innocent after attacking the Lord's anointed one? Surely the Lord will strike Saul down someday, or he will die of old age or in battle.'" (1 Samuel 26:9-10)

If you have to take matters into your own hands to force the will of God in your life, then you're doing it wrong. David already had a promise from God that he would be the next king of Israel. He did not attempt to earn or cajole anyone for this position; God simply promised it to him. All he had to do was wait for it. The problem with waiting is that it can take a while. On two different occasions, David could have killed Saul to speed up the process, but he refused to do so! He instinctively understood that if he forced the matter, he would have to work to maintain it.

If you have to work to get it, then you'll have to work to maintain it. It's better to wait for it. David was not lying around doing nothing while he waited. He spent several years running from Saul, but all the while, he was serving people and growing in his leadership and gifting. It wasn't wasted time in his life; it was preparation.

59

Mind Your Thoughts

"But David kept thinking to himself, 'Someday Saul is going to get me. The best thing I can do is escape to the Philistines. Then Saul will stop hunting for me in Israelite territory, and I will finally be safe.'" (1 Samuel 27:1)

This definitely qualified as one of the lowest points of David's life. It's hard to imagine David being safe in Philistine territory. He conveniently forgot that just a few years earlier, he had killed their greatest warrior, Goliath, and was personally responsible for killing thousands of others.

It's important that you think about what you think about. David convinced himself that moving to the enemy's territory was a good idea. The more he thought about it, the more he justified and rationalized his decision. Your decisions are nothing more than a reflection of your thoughts. That is why it's important for you to carefully consider what you allow into your mind.

60

God's Reward

"The Lord gives his own reward for doing good and for being loyal, and I refused to kill you even when the Lord placed you in my power, for you are the Lord's anointed one." (1 Samuel 26:23)

Once again, David was face-to-face with the man who had attempted to kill him. On this occasion, David refused to kill Saul by taking matters into his own hands. Saul faced a sobering moment when he realized that David could have killed him but chose not to do so. Saul admitted he was wrong and told David he would no longer try to kill him. Saul's reward to David was a promise to stop chasing him so David could move back home (1 Samuel 26:21). However, David knew that if he moved back home, he would be subjecting himself to Saul's abusive power again. Instead, David chose the reward of heaven over the reward of man.

I don't know what reward David experienced, but I suspect it could have been a pure conscience and a good reputation. During this era, to become the king, a son had to inherit the position from his father. The only other alternative was to kill the king and take the position for yourself. David was not a king's son and wasn't about to kill a man to get it. Instead, he chose to trust God and wait.

When you choose to do good to someone who has mistreated you, then there's a reward from heaven. I don't know exactly what that will be, but rest assured, it's better than anything man can give you.

Your Victory Starts With Your Mouth

"The Lord who rescued me from the paw of the lion and the paw of the bear will rescue me from the hand of this Philistine." (1 Samuel 17:37)

D avid had never faced a giant before, but he had faced a lion and a bear. When faced with a new crisis, David recounted his past victories. He reckoned that if God could rescue him once, He would rescue him again. David didn't fixate his attention on the size of the giant, but rather on the size of his God!

When David faced the giant, he understood that the victory started in his mouth before it manifested on the battlefield. You can't have a victorious life with a negative confession. Your victory starts with your mouth. To defeat a giant, you must speak more about your victories than your problems.

62

He Heals Them All

"And whatever their sickness or disease, or if they were demon possessed or epileptic or paralyzed—he healed them all." (Matthew 4:24)

There were no sicknesses or diseases that Jesus could not handle. In every circumstance, He had an answer. His power had no limits! The Gospels record Jesus going to three different funerals. In each situation, He raised the person from the dead. Truthfully, He was bad news for the local funeral homes.

If Jesus can resurrect the dead, He can resurrect any situation in your life. Nothing was too far gone for Him. If you need a miracle in your life, then call on Him today. There's no disease He can't heal. There's no prodigal He can't bring home. There's no marriage He can't save, and there's no debt He can't pay. There's no situation He can't turn around. He specializes in turn-around stories. Go ahead; invite Him to write a new story with your life!

63

Give it Away

"Then Abraham prayed to God, and God healed Abimilech, his wife, and his female servants, so they could have children." (Genesis 20:17)

Let's be honest. It's hard to pray for someone else's miracle while you're waiting for your own miracle, especially if it's what you've been praying to receive. Nonetheless, God honors sowing and reaping—not only in your finances, but also in your prayers. God is not short on miracles. If He can do it for them, then He can do it for you.

It takes faith to give away what you need. Pray for someone else's miracle while you wait for the miracle in your own house. What you make happen for others, God will make happen for you.

64

Faith Requires Work

"Faith without works is dead." (James 2:26)

The greatest evidence of faith is work. When you believe strongly in something, you'll put effort behind it. You don't need to take a giant leap, just a step! It could be a small step, like writing the first sentence of a paragraph. Losing weight begins with taking one lap around your neighborhood. Running a 5K starts with signing up for one. You might desire a greater income. What if you started tithing 11% instead of 10%? God can't bless what you are not doing. At some point, you have to put boots to your prayers. What small step do you need to take?

Discipline is Your Friend

"No discipline seems pleasant at the time, but painful. Later on, however, it produces a harvest of righteousness and peace for those who have been trained by it." (Hebrews 12:11)

Discipline is not meant to be easy. By its nature, it's designed to teach lessons that you do not easily forget. Discipline has to be hard so you learn the lesson and do not repeat the same mistakes over and over again. Initially, discipline is painful, but in the end, it brings peace into your life. Peace comes when you're living in obedience to God and His commands.

66

Think for a Change

"Do not conform to the pattern of this world, but be transformed by the renewing of your mind. Then you will be able to test and approve what God's will is—his good, pleasing and perfect will." (Romans 12:2)

The only way to change your mind is to change your thoughts. When you change your thoughts, you'll change your habits. When you change your habits, you'll change your life.

The best way to start to change your life is by spending time in God's Word. When you spend time in His word, you'll begin to change how you think, and your mind will be renewed. When you renew your mind, everything else will follow suit.

It Matters Who You Follow

"Lot, who was traveling with Abram, had also become very wealthy with flocks of sheep and goats, herds of cattle, and many tents." (Genesis 13:5)

Lot was a scrub. He didn't always make good decisions, but he did get one thing right—he followed Abraham. Lot didn't have the favor and blessing of God that Abraham had on his life, but he was smart enough to follow a man who did. Who you follow and learn from matters! Lot became very wealthy because he chose to follow a man with a vision.

You don't have to have everything figured out or have all the experience, but if you connect with someone who has more experience than you, you can learn from that person. Lot did not have Abraham's business acumen, but he obviously learned a thing or two from his uncle.

Who do you follow? What books do you read? What podcasts do you listen to? Who you follow will determine who you become.

The Messy Middle

"So let's not get tired of doing what is good. At just the right time we will reap a harvest of blessing if we don't give up." (Galatians 6:9)

It's easy to start something new. Good intentions are enough to start something, but it takes consistency and perseverance to finish something. Surviving the messy middle is the hardest part of doing anything for the Lord. Surviving the middle is hard because it takes discipline to keep going when motivation has left the building. It requires you to keep going when you don't feel like it. The only way to achieve anything of significance in your life is to keep showing up. Keep writing that book. Keep lifting those weights. Keep praying the same prayer over and over. Keep on, keeping on. Keep facing it until you make it!

Divine Multiplication

"Five of you will chase a hundred, and a hundred of you will chase ten thousand! All your enemies will fall beneath your sword." (Leviticus 26:8)

There's multiplication in unity. Something happens when people come into agreement together. According to this Scripture, five unified people can chase a hundred enemies away, and a hundred unified people can chase away ten thousand enemies. That's why the enemy uses division as his best strategy to destroy the church. When people are divided, multiplication is lost, but when people work together, multiplication happens.

Jesus affirmed this teaching when He told his disciples, "I also tell you this: If two of you agree here on earth concerning anything you ask, my Father in heaven will do it for you. For where two or three gather together as my followers, I am there among them" (Matthew 18:19-20). Apparently, when Jesus is in your circle, anything can happen.

Don't Forget

"You must observe this festival to the Lord for seven days every year. This is a permanent law for you, and it must be observed in the appointed month from generation to generation. For seven days you must live outside in little shelters. All native-born Israelites must live in shelters. This will remind each new generation of Israelites that I made their ancestors live in shelters when I rescued them from the land of Egypt. I am the Lord your God." (Leviticus 23:41-43)

The Lord never wanted the Israelites to forget that they once lived as captive slaves in Egypt and as wanderers who lived in little shelters in the desert. When they finally entered the Promised Land, they lived in houses they did not build and ate from gardens they did not plant. God brought them from the poorhouse to their own house.

God instituted this yearly festival so parents would teach their children about how far they had come. There's nothing wrong with wanting to give your children the life you didn't have, but don't forget to show them how far you have come. This generates gratitude, and it lets your children know that someone paid a price for them to be where they are today.

He's Saving it for You

"So the cook brought in the meat and placed it before Saul. 'Go ahead and eat it,' Samuel said. 'I was saving it for you even before I invited these others!' So Saul ate with Samuel that day." (1 Samuel 9:24)

Saul was looking for lost donkeys, and Samuel was looking for a king. Saul went to the sacrifice, and what was served to him had already been set aside for him. The only thing he had to do to receive it was to obey and show up. God doesn't keep provision from you; He keeps it for you.

You don't have to worry about the Lord holding anything back from you. He has everything you need, and at just the right time, He will give it to you.

Hard Work

"Work brings profit, but mere talk leads to poverty!" (Proverbs 14:23)

The only place where the reward comes before the work is the dictionary. There's nothing wrong with talking and planning, but at some point, you have to put away the words and pick up a shovel. People who consistently prosper aren't lucky. They've just learned to err on the side of action. They're keenly aware that they won't get everything right, but also realize they only need to get one thing right to hit it big.

Prosperity favors those who take action. You're not going to get every decision right. You are going to make mistakes, but that's part of the process. Don't be afraid to make a mistake; be more afraid of not trying.

Meanwhile

"Meanwhile, the boy Samuel served the Lord by assisting Eli." (1 Samuel 3:1)

S amuel was in a position where he had to serve under someone. He was a young leader who had a prophetic gift in his life and was an anointed leader. It's easy to think that serving the Lord means standing behind a pulpit or leading from a stage, but sometimes the best serving you can do is by assisting someone else. Good or bad, we serve the Lord through leadership, not around it.

Samuel faithfully served Eli, and when the time was right, the Lord raised Samuel up to take his place. When you faithfully serve the Lord, you won't have to worry about the next promotion. The Lord knows where you are and will always find a way to raise you up.

Words and Actions

"Your love for one another will prove to the world that you are my disciples."
(John 13:35)

J esus said that we prove to the world that we are His disciples by how
we love one another. How do we prove that we love others? We
prove it by putting actions to our words. The proof is in our deeds,
not just our words. Society superfluously throws around the word "love,"
but being a doer is what separates you from the talkers. People observe
your actions before they'll listen to your words; in essence, your actions
earn you the right to be heard.

A little kindness goes a long way. It's in such short supply these days
that it doesn't take much to stand out. If you practice it enough, it could
be a superpower. What are some simple things you can do to demonstrate
God's love to others?

Discipline

"A man without self-control is like a city broken into and left without walls."
(Proverbs 25:28)

S elf-control is meant to protect you. To have self-control is to have walls around your life. You cultivate self-control by learning to say "no" to things. Much like a muscle, the more resistance you apply to it, the stronger it becomes. However, the less you use it, the weaker it gets.

When you don't practice self-control, you leave yourself open to the attack of the enemy and vulnerable to your flesh. How can you have more self-control in your life? What do you need to say "no" to more often?

76

Seasons

"For everything there is a season, and a time for every matter under heaven"
(Ecclesiastes 3:1)

D on't mistake a short season for a life sentence. Nothing is going to last forever in your life. It's important to understand your current season of life. When my children were younger, I wanted them to grow up. When I had teenagers, I wanted them to become young adults. When they became adults, I wanted them to be children again. All too often, we want to rush from one season of life to the next.

It's important not to rush the season in which you currently find yourself. Take the time to enjoy the process. Don't be so focused on the goal that you miss the journey. (It pained me to write that sentence!) What season of life are you in? How can you slow down more to enjoy it?

Draw Near

"David was now in great danger because all his men were very bitter about losing their sons and daughters, and they began to talk of stoning him. But David found strength in the Lord his God." (1 Samuel 30:6)

David and his men's families had been ransacked and kidnapped at Ziklag. In their overwhelming grief, David's men talked of stoning him. Hurt people often look for someone to blame for their troubles. However, David didn't play the blame game. He never rebuked his men for wanting to stone him. Instead, he centered himself on God and found strength in his relationship with Him.

Many people are tempted to run away and blame God for their crisis. Not so with David; he drew near during his crisis. After acknowledging his pain and emotions, he prayed to the Lord and asked what to do next.

After praying, the Lord instructed David to go after the Amalekites to get everything back.

If you're facing a crisis today, take time to draw near the Lord and wait for His instructions. You might discover that your setback was a setup for a comeback!

Your Circle Matters

"Some people came, bringing a paralyzed man to Jesus. Four of them were carrying the paralyzed man. But they could not get to Jesus because of the crowd. So they went to the roof above Jesus and made a hole in the roof. Then they lowered the mat with the paralyzed man on it." (Mark 2:3-4)

Your circle of friends matters. You need the kind of friends that would tear the roof off a house to get you to Jesus. While it's probably not a good idea to destroy someone's roof to get you to Jesus, it might be good if your circle of friends would call out to Jesus on your behalf.

If you don't have people in your circle who would do this, then you need to work on your circle. Are you this kind of friend for someone? Who do you need to add to your circle?

The Only Vote That Counts

"This letter is from Paul, an apostle. I was not appointed by any group of people or any human authority, but by Jesus Christ himself and by God the Father, who raised Jesus from the dead." (Galatians 1:1)

Paul's calling to be an apostle did not come through a committee or a vote of confidence. It came through the Lord Jesus Christ himself. It wasn't based on the opinion of others. In fact, it wasn't even based on Paul's opinion of himself. Man can recognize our calling and see God's call on our lives. However, they can't give it to us, and they can't take it away. Only Jesus has that authority! Man votes; God calls.

If you're waiting on man's approval to attempt something for God, you might be waiting a long time. Now is the time to get moving. Jesus has already voted for you; His vote is the only one that counts!

80

Generosity Always Wins

"But generous people plan to do what is generous, and they stand firm in their generosity." (Isaiah 32:8)

Generous people are purposeful and intentional about their giving. They're not swayed by their emotions or motivated by greed. They can stand firm in their generosity because they trust the Lord, not their wallets. This past year, my wife and I wanted to be more purposeful in our giving, so we started setting giving goals, not getting goals. This changed everything for us because now we plan our giving, making giving more purposeful and fun. We also understand that God supplies seed to the sower, not the hoarder (2 Corinthians 9:10). What are you planning to sow into today?

81

Big Expectations

"All praise to God, the Father of our Lord Jesus Christ. It is by his great mercy that we have been born again, because God raised Jesus Christ from the dead. Now we live with great expectation, and we have a priceless inheritance—an inheritance that is kept in heaven for you, pure and undefiled, beyond the reach of change and decay." (1 Peter 1:3-4)

What are you expecting? Are you expecting good or bad in your life? It's easy to be pessimistic and always be looking for the shoe to drop or to expect the worst. As a believer, we don't have to live this way. We are people of faith and can expect good things from God. Hebrews 11:1 says, "Faith shows the reality of what we hope for; it is the evidence of things we cannot see." When you have faith, there is always hope in your life. Keep praying, keep hoping, and keep believing because when God is writing your story, there's always a surprise ending!

It's the Little Things

"So Naaman went with his horses and chariots and waited at the door of Elisha's house. But Elisha sent a messenger out to him with this message: 'Go and wash yourself seven times in the Jordan River. Then your skin will be restored, and you will be healed of your leprosy.'" (2 Kings 5:9-10)

Naaman was a big deal. He brought his entourage of horses and chariots to Elisha's house. Naaman knocked on the door and waited, but Elisha wasn't moved by his fame. Instead, he sent a servant to the door to pass along his message. Naaman took this as an insult and stalked away. This sounded too simple to him. He wanted to see the spectacular. He wanted to see a show. He was expecting something hard, not something simple.

This is a good reminder that God often prefers the mundane of simple obedience. There was nothing spectacular about the Jordan River. In like manner, we often pass on the little things because we are too busy looking for the spectacular. God just might be looking for our simple obedience before He does the spectacular. Where is He waiting on you to be obedient in your life?

The Entitlement Trap

"But Gehazi, the servant of Elisha, the man of God, said to himself, 'My master should not have let this Arabian get away without accepting any of his gifts. As surely as the Lord lives, I will chase after him and get something from him.' So Gehazi set off after Naaman." (2 Kings 5:20-21)

As an Aramean, the people of Israel considered Naaman as unclean and as an enemy. He came to Elisha looking for healing; when he was healed, he offered to reward him for his time. Under normal circumstances, it would not be wrong to accept a gift, but Elisha told Gehazi that this was not the time. Elisha was teaching Naaman that you cannot buy grace; it is a free gift. Gehazi lost sight of his calling and thought Naaman owed him something. The moment you feel like people owe you something, you're in trouble. Entitlement will lead to your downfall.

84

Don't be Impatient

"While Elisha was still saying this, the messenger arrived. And the king said, 'All this misery is from the Lord! Why should I wait for the Lord any longer?'"
(2 Kings 6:33)

The king of Israel grew impatient with the Lord's deliverance. His impatience morphed into rage, and he sent people to kill Elisha. In essence, he was looking for someone to blame, and Elisha was his target. In the end, God protected Elisha, and he prophesied their deliverance.

It's easy to get upset and blame the Lord while you're waiting on your miracle. Our pain and frustration can be misdirected if we aren't careful. It's never a good thing to blame God, especially when He's the only one that can deliver us. The only thing worse than waiting is wishing you had. Where do you need to keep waiting on the Lord?

The Potter's Shop

"The Lord gave another message to Jeremiah. He said, 'Go down to the potter's shop, and I will speak to you there.' So I did as he told me and found the potter working at his wheel. But the jar he was making did not turn out as he had hoped, so he crushed it into a lump of clay again and started over."
(Jeremiah 18:1-4)

God told Jeremiah to go down to the potter's shop, where He would speak to him. As Jeremiah watched the potter working at his wheel, he saw him mold and shape the clay in his hands. Before a piece of clay becomes something valuable, the potter has to shape it. Every beautiful vase starts out as a clump of clay in the potter's hands.

A lump of clay only becomes valuable and useful as the potter molds and shapes the clay. The pressure from the master potter's hands smooth off the rough edges, but the potter must know the amount of pressure to apply. Too much pressure causes the clay to fold in on itself, while too little pressure results in an uneven and rough pot.

Occasionally, as the potter molds a lump of clay, it does not turn out as he had hoped. In that case, he crushes the clay and starts over. Notice that he does not throw out the clay and label it as a lost cause. No, he applies a little water to soften it in his hands and keeps applying pressure until it becomes what he intends.

At times, we sense the Master Potter working on our lives in much the same way. Maybe you feel like the Potter is crushing you today. If so, you are in good hands. If He's crushing you, it's only because He wants to make something beautiful out of your life. He wants you to be a container of living water that gives life and refreshes those around you.

86

Be Great

"But a beautiful cedar palace does not make a great king! Your father, Josiah, also had plenty to eat and drink. But he was just and right in all his dealings. That is why God blessed him." (Jeremiah 22:15)

You are not great because of what you have. You are great because of Who you serve. King Josiah was one of the last great kings of Israel. He used his throne and platform to serve those around him. He used his authority to serve the poor and needy. He spoke up for those who could not speak for themselves. Josiah used his kingship to serve God and his people. On the other hand, Jehoiakim used his kingship to build something for himself. While building his great palace, Jehoiakim used forced labor and exploited the poor in the process.

We do not measure the greatness of a man by what he has, but in what he gives. Greatness is not measured in houses or cars, but in who we are and Who we serve. What do you want to be remembered for?

Dry Seasons

"For this is what the Lord, the God of Israel, says: 'There will always be flour and olive oil left in your containers until the time when the Lord sends rain and the crops grow again!'" (1 Kings 17:14)

While living in a season of famine, the widow felt like she had nothing left to give or share. Truthfully, she only had enough for one more day. Elijah came along and promised her that she would have flour and oil left in her containers until the famine subsided.

Even when we feel dry and empty, we can believe that God will fill us with all we need and help us give to others who need the bread of life. When the widow stepped out in faith to feed Elijah, each new day there was always enough in her jar to feed her and her entire family. You have enough for one more day.

Your Future is in Good Hands

"But I am trusting you, O Lord, saying, 'You are my God!' My future is in your hands. Rescue me from those who hunt me down relentlessly." (Psalm 31:14-15)

Do you ever worry about the future? Do you ever find yourself worrying about a family member? Maybe a son or a daughter? If so, you're in good company! Even King David worried from time to time. When he found himself worrying, he would remind himself who his God was. He would say to himself, "You are my God!"

If you worry about the future, I encourage you to commit these two verses to memory. Like David, say them out loud. Recite them back to yourself and personalize them. Put your name in the text and repeat it. If you're worried about a family member, then personalize the Scripture with his or her name and declare it aloud. Scriptures become prayers when we verbalize them.

Quit Making Excuses

"The lazy person claims, 'There's a lion out there! If I go outside, I might be killed!'" (Proverbs 22:13)

L azy people make excuses, while diligent people make a way. You'll find an excuse or find a way, but you can't do both. A lot of people are afraid to attempt something new because they're afraid of what might go wrong. Sure, you might encounter dangers when trying something new, but I believe the cost of staying the same is more dangerous. Mistakes are going to happen. That is just part of life— part of the growing process. Don't be afraid of making mistakes; be more afraid of not trying. The more you try, the more you're bound to succeed. You can't succeed at what you don't try.

You Probably Shouldn't

"'All things are lawful for me,' but not all things are helpful. 'All things are lawful for me,' but I will not be dominated by anything." (1 Corinthians 6:12)

Y ou can do many things, but not all of these things are a good idea! My mind says I am twenty-five, but my body says otherwise! You must decide where you will place the line on certain things. For example, alcohol consumption: Scripture indicates that drinking alcohol is not a sin, but admonishes one not to get drunk. However, just because drinking is not a sin, does not mean it is a good idea. Over the years, I have personally seen too many people in my family get in trouble because of the abuse of alcohol. Consequently, my wife and I made the personal decision not to drink. I'm also cheap and would prefer to spend my money on something else!

Just because you can, does not mean you should. In which areas of your life do you need to draw a line? What can others do that you probably shouldn't do? Only you can answer this question for yourself.

BONUS DAY

Walk Through It

"Then Moses raised his hand over the sea, and the Lord opened up a path through the water with a strong east wind. The wind blew all that night, turning the seabed into dry land. So the people of Israel walked through the middle of the sea on dry ground, with walls of water on each side!" (Exodus 14:21-22)

When we face problems, our first response is usually to ask the Lord to remove the problem. I've lived long enough to recognize that He doesn't always do it like I think He should. He usually has something different in mind.

When facing an obstacle, it's essential to keep your eyes open to what the Lord might want to do. Just because you've never seen it done before, doesn't mean He can't do it. God likes to create new things, and He is not going to run out of miracles. For that matter, He rarely does the same thing the same way. He likes variety. God didn't remove the Red Sea; He parted it. God doesn't always remove your problems, but He will make a way through them.

ADDITIONAL RESOURCES

Prayerfully, this book ministered to you in some way. It's our hope that you would continue in your faith journey. You can sign up to receive a free daily devotional that can be read in under two minutes. You can sign up at Eric's website at www.ericspeir.com.

This book operates on the premise that God loves you and wants to be actively involved in your life. Maybe your life has been a struggle, and you have never made a decision for Christ, or maybe it's been a long time since you've talked to him. You can take a moment today and invite Jesus into your life. If you want this, then you can use this prayer as a guide:

Lord Jesus, I confess my sins and ask for your forgiveness. Please come into my heart as my Lord and Savior. Take complete control of my life and help me to walk in Your footsteps daily by the power of the Holy Spirit. Thank you Lord for saving me and for answering my prayer. In Jesus' name. Amen.

If you would like additional prayer for your life, please feel free to send a prayer request to eric@ericspeir.com. Eric and his wife would love to hear from you and would commit to praying for your family as well.

ABOUT THE AUTHOR

Eric Speir is a serial encourager, writer, pastor, and Bible college professor. His goal is to restore hope where it's been lost. Eric holds a doctor of ministry degree in leadership development and creative communication. He and his wife, Roshelle, have four children and live near Atlanta, Georgia.

You can find out more information about Eric and his other writing projects through his website at www.ericspeir.com.

If this book ministered to you in some way, we would love for you to leave a review on Amazon! You can also email us at Eric@ericspeir.com.

COMING SOON BY ERIC S. SPEIR

Fresh Fire: 90 Quick Read Devotionals Book Two (Jan. 2024)

Fresh Fire: 90 Quick Read Devotionals Book Three (April 2024)

Fresh Fire: 90 Quick Read Devotionals Book Four (July 2024)